YOU ARE
MORE
THAN ORDINARY

Ordinary Kids • Royal Identity • Divine Purpose

Published by
You Are More Press
Georgetown, TX

Paperback ISBN: 979-87662916-1-9
Hardcover ISBN: 979-8-9850433-0-3

Illustrations by Ariel Arriaga

And a huge thank you to those who helped with the production of You Are More Than Ordinary: Zach, Josh, and Danielle. I'm so grateful that God has put you in my life.

Printed in the United States

YOU ARE MORE

You are a chosen people, a royal priesthood, a holy nation, a people belonging to God, that you may declare the praises of him who called you out of darkness into his wonderful light.

1 Peter 2:9

God's Superpower Love for You!

Each book in the "You are More" series shows how Jesus' love for us makes us MORE than ordinary kids. As you read the story, listen for the word "superpower love" and look for the crown, cape and armor on David, Liam and Katherine. God gives you this invisible armor when he gives you faith in Jesus. You can read about these powerful truths for you in God's Word before you start the story.

Super Power Love:

For Christ's love compels us, because we are convinced that one died for all and therefore all died.
2 Corinthians 5:4

Jesus died to be with us forever because he loves us. His love is so powerful that it makes us want to love like him.

The Crown:

But you are a chosen people, a royal priesthood, a holy nation, a people belonging to God, that you may declare the praises of him who called you out of darkness into his wonderful light.
1 Peter 2:9

We are royal children of the King of Kings! We are his priesthood, the messengers of Jesus' love. The two terms: **royal children** and **royal priesthood** give us two very important blessings: **identity and purpose.**

The Armor:

Finally, be strong in the Lord and in his mighty power.
Put on the full armor of God so that you can take your stand against the devil's schemes.
Ephesians 6:10-11

The truth that Jesus died to forgive us all of our sin is our protection from Satan's attacks. Jesus knows we cannot fight temptation and sin with our own efforts. He has fought that battle for us on the cross.

The White Cape:

God made him who had no sin to be sin for us,
so that in him we might become the righteousness of God.
2 Corinthians 5:21

Jesus took away the mess of our sin and gave us his identity. When God looks at us, he sees us wearing the purity of Jesus like a white robe or cape.

4

Come here, Katherine! Come here, Liam!

9

Do you think your life is too ordinary? I want to show you something I did that made it special.

I love you! I died for you! That means that you are much more than any superhero or princess!

and you are my royal children!

13

Do you see?
My love for you is my **super power**...

14

And guess what? When you trust my love, my superpower love lives in you!

15

"But I don't look any different."

No you don't, but you are.

Let me tell you a story about David.

He looked like an ordinary kid, too.

But David knew he was God's child! David knew God loved him! And **that** made him more than ordinary!

20

One day, a mean giant named Goliath wanted to hurt God's people.

Everyone except David. David knew that Goliath could be defeated.

23

because David knew God was with him!

David ran up to Goliath with only a sling and five stones.

26

Trusting God's help, he put a stone in the sling and swung it around and around.

And then he let it go...
The stone sailed through the air and

smacked Goliath right in the head!

Goliath dropped to the ground
like a big tree and died.

29

All the people saw the **power of God** who saved them from Goliath using an ordinary kid.

I love to save people.

My love is my superpower that saves you.

My superpower love fills you with love to share! Katherine and Liam, you are like David who I used to save people from Goliath.

You are more than ordinary kids.

When you tell other people how much I love them...

My superpower love saves them, too!

Because I love you so much I want to be with you forever! Nothing can keep you away from my love. No hurt, no bad things you've done.

You are very, very special to me.
You are more than an ordinary kid.

The story of David and Goliath is found in 1 Samuel 17. God used David, a boy, who was much younger and smaller than his enemies, to save his people. David knew he was God's child. He knew God could rescue his people from Goliath and the Philistines. That love of God was David's super power to trust God and fight Goliath. Like David, we are more than ordinary even though we do not look like it. We have an extraordinary purpose to share the message that God loved the world so much that he sent his Son, Jesus, to save us. And, like David, God's love is our super power that gives us the power to trust him and do his work.

Jesus teaches us about our true identity and purpose in him. Use this book as a conversation starter with your family.

What did Katherine and Liam wish they were? What is exciting about being a princess? What is exciting about being a superhero?

What did Jesus say you are?

How would you feel if you had to fight a giant like Goliath?

What did David know that helped him in his fight?

What's a time when you've felt like the boy David as he faced a giant?

God tells you that you are his child. He's the King of Kings, and you're his son or daughter! How does that make you feel when you face scary or challenging things?

You are a child of the king and have his superpower love. God has given you a job of using that love to help others. What is a way that you can use his love to help someone?

About the Author

Chris creates illustrated children's books that communicate the truth of Jesus's unconditional love for families. Her YOU ARE MORE Christian Children's Book series emphasizes that God gives us his identity and purpose as his dearly loved children. Chris lives in Georgetown, TX with her husband Allan and whatever birds they can attract to their backyard feeders.

About the Illustrator

Ariel simply loves to draw, and is fascinated with the boundless creativity that the universe unfolds itself to us in. Blessed with the opportunity to put forth her ever-changing talent in a way that sustains many dreams, she's adopted this challenge to convey messages from the Bible into a children's book series with extreme love and playfulness! She has discovered many new frontiers in the production of this work, and is humbled to share what she can offer to the world as the series continues.

Made in the USA
Las Vegas, NV
02 January 2025

15739830R00026